MW01064765

PRISON BOOK PROJECT
P.O. BOX 1146
Sharpes, FL 32959

A Final Experiment

*A Simple, Direct, and Personal
Formula to Connect with God*

Tom Stegeman

WESTBOW
PRESS®
A DIVISION OF THOMAS NELSON
& ZONDERVAN

Copyright © 2021 Tom Stegeman.

All rights reserved. No part of this book may be used or reproduced
by any means, graphic, electronic, or mechanical, including
photocopying, recording, taping or by any information storage
retrieval system without the written permission of the author except in
the case of brief quotations embodied in critical articles and reviews.

WestBow Press books may be ordered through
booksellers or by contacting:

WestBow Press
A Division of Thomas Nelson & Zondervan
1663 Liberty Drive
Bloomington, IN 47403
www.westbowpress.com
844-714-3454

Because of the dynamic nature of the Internet, any web
addresses or links contained in this book may have changed
since publication and may no longer be valid. The views
expressed in this work are solely those of the author and do
not necessarily reflect the views of the publisher, and the
publisher hereby disclaims any responsibility for them.

Any people depicted in stock imagery provided by Getty Images are
models, and such images are being used for illustrative purposes only.
Certain stock imagery © Getty Images.

ISBN: 978-1-6642-1557-3 (sc)
ISBN: 978-1-6642-1558-0 (e)

Library of Congress Control Number: 2020924099

Printed in the United States of America.

WestBow Press rev. date: 01/19/2021

This book is a work of non-fiction. Unless otherwise noted, the author and the publisher make no explicit guarantees as to the accuracy of the information contained in this book and in some cases, names of people and places have been altered to protect their privacy.

Scripture quotations marked (AMP) are taken from the Amplified Bible, Copyright © 1954, 1958, 1962, 1964, 1965, 1987 by The Lockman Foundation. Used by permission.

Scripture marked (NKJV) taken from the New King James Version®. Copyright © 1982 by Thomas Nelson. Used by permission. All rights reserved.

Scripture quotations marked (NIV) are taken from the Holy Bible, New International Version®, NIV®. Copyright © 1973, 1978, 1984, 2011 by Biblica, Inc.® Used by permission of Zondervan. All rights reserved worldwide. www.zondervan.com The "NIV" and "New International Version" are trademarks registered in the United States Patent and Trademark Office by Biblica, Inc.®

Scripture quotations marked CSB have been taken from the Christian Standard Bible®, Copyright © 2017 by Holman Bible Publishers. Used by permission. Christian Standard Bible® and CSB® are federally registered trademarks of Holman Bible Publishers.

CONTENTS

PREFACE

Once, someone ask me a *simple, direct*
question: "Did you know that you could
have a personal relationship with God?"

I replied, "No?"

"Would you like that?"

I said, "Yes."

And that is why I've written this book.

ACKNOWLEDGMENTS

I want to give a tremendous thank-you to the following people who helped me accomplish this book.

My wife, Ellen, not only reedited this book several times but also allowed me to put off a few house projects so that I could finish it.

Dr. Sara (Sally) Johnson Worley is my spiritual big sister who initiated my spiritual journey when I first became a Christian.

Jim Holbrook of McGregor Baptist Church, Fort Myers, Florida (retired), has been my pastor and good friend since 1978.

Bob Fain is a long-time friend as well as an inspirational Bible study teacher.

Pete Adams helped me with this book, even though he was battling terminal cancer.

Mark Siverling and Bill Nunez. Two great Christian brothers.

Young Life Ministries. A truly awesome outreach for teenagers.

Most of all, I want to thank my Lord and Savior for inspiring me to tell my story.

Please search A Final Experiment on the web or social media for further information regarding this book, its author and additional reference materials.

INTRODUCTION

Do you feel like you're important? I believe that most of us have an innate desire to feel admired by others. Maybe we would like to accomplish something in life that would leave a lasting mark showing who we are. Even if we don't outwardly admit it, I believe that our basic nature is to think that we only have one life to live and that we must make it count for something. Why else would we be trying so hard to find our self-worth?

So what would your ultimate motive be in satisfying this need? Would it be to earn a lot of money, become a celebrity, or to win a Nobel Prize? How about being a political leader or a famous artist or writer?

Many of us think that these things would leave marks on society, which other people would admire. In other words, we've convinced ourselves that if we could somehow feel important to ourselves and others, it would be the ultimate satisfaction in our lives. However, the reality for most of us will be that we lived never fulfilling this desire. Maybe if we're lucky, a few family members and friends will say that we were pretty good people when we're gone.

You see, I believe there is a *God-shaped* hole in us that can only be filled by God. Psalm 139:13 (AMP) says, "For You formed my innermost parts." This may sound strange, but think about it—we're constantly trying to fill or satisfy our inner needs with things or accomplishments. Most of the things that we strive for take tremendous amounts of time and effort and sometimes still don't satisfy or fill this void.

Think about the people in history who have accomplished something important during their lives. Many of them were still not completely satisfied with their lives. Their lives often ended sadly in some disaster.

My point is that you probably want your life to be meaningful or count for something. At some point, you would like to feel that you are an important part of this world. What if this were possible and easy? That is what I am proposing in this book. What if instead of achievements or others making us feel important, God made us feel that way?

I can personally tell you that as soon as I asked God to save me (see the "My Story" chapter) and His spirit entered the place that was reserved for Him inside me, I felt like the most important person that had ever walked the earth. I no longer needed another person's praise or to prove anything to anyone. My self-worth was fully satisfied. I instantly became a King's kid.

Does this sound ridiculous to you? Good. It did to me at first also. If you can hang in there and get through this book, you may find, as I did, a whole new outlook on life.

I have tried to make all the topics and ideas as clear and simple as possible. That is why I've subtitled the book *A Simple, Direct, and Personal Formula to Connect with God.*

MY STORY

From age two to eighteen, I lived in a very exclusive, upper-middle-class suburb of Cincinnati, Ohio. I was two years old in 1957 and eighteen in 1973, the year I graduated high school. Basically, my whole upbringing was isolated to the same surroundings, friends, and families, which I got to know very well. Most of the people in our community were living the American dream on steroids.

Looking back, it was a pretty amazing childhood for me and my two brothers, particularly in the early years. Mom and Dad were about as all-American and good looking as June and Ward Cleaver on one of our favorite

TV shows. Would you believe that their real names are Barbie and Ken? I'm not making that up. Everything was great in the early years. Dad was our baseball coach. Mom was our Cub Scout leader and usually involved with several community groups and school organizations.

By the time I was six, our perfect lives took a drastic turn. Some difficult situations entered our perfect household. For starters, my older brother (by eighteen months), Scott, was diagnosed with cerebral palsy as a toddler. He was slow to walk and continued to have a slight limp in his step throughout his life. His left side was also affected. He had limited use of his left hand and arm. I know this was a hard thing for Mom and Dad to handle, but they did their best to provide a normal childhood for him.

Things took an even worse turn for Scott when in first grade he had a grand mal seizure. There was no warning, and he had it in his classroom. Paramedics rushed him to the hospital. Mom and Dad didn't know what was going on, and they thought they were going to lose him. Scott came out of it fine, but he was diagnosed with severe epilepsy. Scott's life had become a small crack in our otherwise perfect family.

Then when I was around ten years old, we were shocked when our parents told us that they were getting a divorce. Still being a young boy, I was in shock. I didn't understand the reasons why then, and I still don't fully know now, some fifty years later. This was a very traumatic event for us boys, as it would be for most kids whose parents separate. You have to realize that in 1965, it was rare to hear the word *divorce*. It was considered a social taboo back then. Mom took over most of the parenting responsibilities because Dad was in and out of our lives during most of our adolescent years.

Why am I starting off with all this personal background? Because I want you to know that even though I started life with a silver spoon in my mouth, that spoon soon tarnished. I grew up with good and bad experiences. At times, we had plenty, and at others, we struggled to make ends meet. I want you to know that I can relate to almost anyone's life situation because of the life I have lived.

It's interesting that many of the difficult situations that occurred in my early years turned me from depending on my parents for security to wondering if God could help me sort things out. Maybe God cared about me and my family. I prayed often, asking Him to help us. I continued to wonder if my life meant anything to anyone, including God. This brings me to my next subject.

My Religious Background

While growing up, we attended a local Protestant church. It was a beautiful church. The exterior was a traditional limestone block structure. The inside was adorned with beautiful cathedral-style wooden arches and large stained-glass windows. The choir loft was behind the two main pulpits. An organ with a huge set of organ pipes was the backdrop, and it went across the entire wall. Do you get the picture? I mean, if I were God, I would be impressed, and I might want to live there.

While growing up, we went to God's house to visit Him every Sunday. However, I never actually saw Him there—ever. It was very confusing. Back then, most of my religious education and what I understood about God came from observing my parents. I watched and listened to their comments and ideas of who God was and how He operated. I caught a lot of religious reality, as I called it, by observing my parents and others at church.

Most Sundays, before and after the service, the men discussed their golf games or the recent football scores while the women talked about their bridge clubs or upcoming PTA meetings. No one ever mentioned what was said in the sermon, even though everyone complimented the pastor on his inspirational message as they greeted him leaving the church service.

I look back and realize that attendance at our church, which may be like yours, was part of being socially correct. Our church was more of a country club than a church. It was just another place to gather and be seen doing the right thing by your peers. We wanted to be accepted by the church, its leaders, our friends, and maybe even God. All this only further confused me. Where was God in all of it? Was this all there was to having a relationship with Him?

On my end, Sundays were horrible. We understood that we had to get up every day for school, but we wondered why we had to get up on one of our days off to go to Sunday school. To make things worse, we had to dress up to go visit God. I remember wearing a little sports jacket and a tie. Thank God for the guy who invented the clip-on tie. We looked like little insurance salesmen. I often wondered why we couldn't just wear our regular school clothes. Did God really care how we dressed? Apparently, He did. This was just another confusing concept about God and church for me. To this day, I only dress up if

I absolutely have to. I think some therapy could have helped me on this one.

Going to Sunday school was a whole other issue. First, we had to dress up in our stiff-as-a-board coats, which were like straightjackets. Second, I wondered why we had to go to another school. We had already gone to our regular school five days that week.

After finally getting to church, we settled into our classrooms. Then the teacher proceeded to tell us some outrageous story from the Bible for almost half an hour, like the story of Noah and the Ark. Did they really expect us to believe that a man spent forty years building a boat? Did they expect us to believe that two of every animal on the planet showed up at the same place and time and that they all got along?

We never got an answer from the teacher as to what the story meant. The answer from our teacher usually was, "Well, this is the story we had on the Sunday school calendar for this week." We then finished our class time by pasting dried elbow-macaroni noodles to a paper plate in the shape of the Ark and drew all the animals in with crayons. This was obviously a time-filler for our teacher.

After church, we met up with our parents. They were excited to hear about the story our teacher had told us and to see the beautiful artwork that we had done (which usually stayed on the refrigerator for a month to remind us of the whole miserable experience). The only good thing that I remember was the paste tasting pretty good and being able to get a little buzz if you ate enough of it.

This Sunday school routine went on during my entire youth. My brothers and I used to love it when my parents either had a party or went to one on a Saturday night. This meant that there was a good chance that they would sleep in on Sunday morning, which meant that we wouldn't have to go to church. Even if they didn't go out Saturday evening, we figured out that if we were really quiet Sunday morning, they might oversleep. If they woke up any time after 8:05 a.m., it would be too late to get ready for church and make it there by 9:00 a.m. It meant no straightjackets, no ties, and no boring Sunday school lessons.

Unfortunately, sleeping in was not the norm. I did not see an end to this ritual until I was thirteen. That year, my parents announced that we would be going to a confirmation class. I personally did not see the need for me to go to a class where they confirmed the brainwashing that I had already received. But apparently, you had to take this class to join the church. Can you imagine my level of enthusiasm?

But then I thought, *Wait, this is my opportunity to quit going to church. I'll intentionally fail the class. They won't confirm me and let me join the church. Problem solved. What a plan!* But guess what? It didn't work. I tried so hard too. I answered every question wrong.

Question: Who was in charge of building the Ark?
Answer: Moses

Question: Name one of the twelve disciples.
Answer: Richard Nixon

My teacher said, "Tom, you don't seem to be trying very hard?"
I thought, *What was your first clue?*

They confirmed me anyway. To add insult to injury, they gave me a box with a whole year's supply of offering envelopes. I thought, *What kind of racket is this?* Did they really think I was going to give the church 10 percent of my measly twenty-dollar-per-week lawn-mowing money?

My next thought was, *If I'm now a member, I can make my own decisions on whether I want to go to church or not.* However, I reluctantly decided to go to church because my mom wanted to go. I felt bad if she went alone. By this time, she was a single mom. My two brothers and I wanted to help support her wishes, which was for all of us to continue to go to church together.

I now got to go to the "big church", as I called

it. I heard things occasionally that sparked my interest in all this God stuff. So I decided that if I had to go, I might as well give it a shot and see if I could figure out why everyone wanted to come every Sunday. Unfortunately, it was pretty much the same message every week: "Be nice to your neighbor," and, "Smell the roses along the way." Week after week, we heard the same flowery themes.

It got to the point where I thought, *Don't you have something else to tell us about God?* I was also still struggling with the concept that we had to go to church if we wanted to visit God. Where was He the rest of the week? Who was this Jesus guy? Why did he keep referring to Him as the Son of God? Could someone please explain this? Nope, they couldn't. So I remained confused about organized religion.

Now don't get me wrong. I wasn't against there being a supreme someone in charge of the universe whom most of us referred to as God. That wasn't my problem. I just wanted to know exactly who He was, where He was, and how I personally fit into His plans. Was that asking too much?

I wasn't sure that I had a problem with God's existence. I had seen enough answers to prayers to know that He probably was around somewhere. But no one—not Mom, Dad, my Sunday school teachers, or my pastors—ever gave me any solid information on how a real relationship with God worked. This was probably because they either didn't know themselves or thought that they did and that we all had our own avenues of getting closer to God.

What I wound up doing throughout my teenage years was going on a spiritual journey alone. I was reasonably sure there was a God. I not only felt that He heard my prayers, but as I said, I saw that many of them had been answered, especially the ones that were not selfish. Regarding most of my answers to prayers, I felt like God wanted me to know that He was there and that He was someone who really cared about the things that were going on in my life. So I did feel that somehow, He was around.

What struck me as funny was that I was getting more out of my own trials and errors while in my bedroom praying to God in my pj's than I had when I had dressed up and gone to church once a week.

This is what I had observed so far as a young teenager:

1) I knew that I was going to a *social-priority-minded* church. I wondered what other churches and religions did.

2) My church was a *generational* religion. My parents decided what my beliefs would be. I found out that my Catholic and Jewish friends were under the same predestined situation.

3) My only real spiritual experience was my personal prayer time. I wasn't sure if any church or organized religion was necessary for me to have a relationship with God.

4) I felt like I was at least being real to myself. No one was going to push their religious concepts on me just because my family had approved it. I was always open to other people's beliefs and other religious concepts that might be deep and meaningful. But up to this point, I never saw or heard any that sparked my interest.

I continued to go to church on rare occasions. I wasn't getting any new revelations from our pastors. It was as if the whole service was predetermined by some national church council, which dictated exactly what was to be read, sung, and preached each week.

I can still remember the order of our services. There was opening organ music with a verbal prelude. The congregation participated in the prayer. We sang the first hymn (all four verses). An Old Testament selection was read, which sometimes sounded fairly interesting, but it was never referred to in the sermon. We sang another hymn (all five verses). There was a solo. Then the pastor preached his sermon: "Be nice to your neighbor," and, "Smell the roses along the way."

I was always amazed at how many ways he could present this same message week after week. Then as everyone walked out, I remember the small exhales from most church members as if to say, "Boy, I'm glad that's over." I was starting to see that others weren't too interested in attending church either.

Speaking of interesting. In order to keep my sanity, I amused myself by looking at all the small details of formal church. Here is an example. I realized that most religious leaders (pastors, priests, and rabbis) wore very specific robes, hats, etc. to identify themselves as leaders in their particular sect of God's army. Our pastor wore a black graduation-style robe with a purple-and-gold sash. The robe also had three purple stripes on each sleeve. I guess that meant he was a captain or maybe a lieutenant colonel.

I was curious as to how one obtained all these official symbols of status. However, I did not want to be recruited. So much of what I saw was just part of a man-made religion. What did God think of all this? In God's eyes, was this church leader more important than I was? Should I be trying to work my way up in the ranks of God's army?

The most confusing thing about what I was hearing was this: I was told that we were all going to heaven because we had been baptized, been confirmed, done the sacraments, or had a bar mitzvah. All these things were different ceremonies that supposedly guaranteed our entry. I wondered, *Are all these tickets accepted by God?*

I felt depressed that I might have to work to achieve some level of approval from God. Did we get into heaven by having good church attendance or checking off all the right boxes on God's to-do list?

After many years of not wanting to go to church anymore, when I reached high school, Mom gave in and left the choice up to us. Guess what I chose to do.

My Salvation Story

I had just turned seventeen. It was my junior year in high school. In spring of 1972, our high school choir was on a bus heading for the annual state high school choir competition. We had collected our usual first place hardware in almost every category. We were heading home after a long, successful day.

On the way home, I wound up sitting with Sally, a senior friend of mine. We knew each other pretty well, as we had both been on the same swim team in the summer. Our families also knew each other well from church and other community activities. Sally's mother was Mom's big sister at their college sorority. Sally was always like a big sister to me.

It was about a three-hour bus ride home. Sally had a captive audience the whole way home—me! She decided to share her story with me. That she had prayed to receive Jesus into her heart. Sally explained how different and great her life had become since that decision. She obviously wanted me to have this same experience. I shared some of my personal thoughts about God with her.

Sally encouraged me because she had experienced some of the same thoughts before she had sorted out this *salvation* thing. Since we both grew up in the same church, we could relate to our religious upbringing very well. I really wasn't sure what she meant when she talked about her prayer of salvation. But I could see that she was sincere about it. She felt that she had finally connected with God through this prayer.

She told me this had been a recent event and that it was a little difficult to explain exactly how it worked and how it happened. I caught more than I heard. The peace, happiness, and satisfaction that were in her voice and attitude were definitely something that I didn't have. It was somehow very appealing to me. This whole conversation stuck with me. Deep down inside, I wanted what she had.

During the last month of that school year, Sally kept bugging me to go to a Young Life meeting, where I could hear what she had been learning about God, Jesus, and salvation. I had been so turned off by church that I had refused to go to any kind of organized program. But she eventually talked me into going to one of its camps that was in June at Saranac Lake, New York.

At first, I was hesitant to tell her that I would go, but she persistently told me how much fun it had been when she had gone the previous summer. I finally said that I would go. She was so excited—much more than I was.

I wasn't sure what I was in for. For that matter, it suddenly occurred to me that I hadn't even gone to a single Young Life meeting. There were all kinds of meetings during the week, and I had been invited to them from time to time. Maybe I should have checked them out first. It was too late now. I was off to camp.

Off to Camp

I showed up at a church across town where we would be leaving for camp. Kids from different

19

Young Life groups in Cincinnati were showing up as well. I didn't know a single person there. I didn't even know the five freshmen girls from my high school that were coming with us. I felt very alone and thought that I had made a huge mistake by telling Sally that I would do it.

I only knew one name. I was to look for a man named Gil, who was the head counselor on the trip. Actually, Gil found me. Sally must have clued him in on my situation, and it's hard to miss a six-foot-five-inch redhead in a crowd.

I wasn't greeted by anyone at first. So I just followed some of the other kids that were already getting on the bus. They were together in small groups. They knew one another and seemed to want to sit toward the back of the bus. Since I didn't know anyone, I decided to just take a seat in the front of the bus. This would also make it easier for Gil to find me. As I sat there by myself, I contemplated getting off and calling Mom to come pick me up.

My negative thoughts were interrupted by a

man's voice, which said, "Hi, I'm Gil. You must be Tom, Sally's friend."

I quickly said, "Oh, hi. Yes, I'm Tom."

Gil sat down beside me, and I'm sure he could instantly sense my nervousness. He took this time to help me feel welcomed and more comfortable about being the new kid on the block. He left getting everyone situated on the bus to the other leaders.

Shortly, Gil started some chitchat about camp.

Gil: "Are you excited about going to camp?"
Me: "Sure."

Gil: "You know, there are so many neat things to do at camp. Most kids can't even decide which one they want to do first. There's volleyball, waterskiing, parasailing, swimming, and basketball. And the food! Wait 'til you taste all the delicious meals that they serve."
Me: "Great."

Gil: "Sally told me a lot about you. She said she thought this would be a great experience for you.

21

Me: "I hope so."

Gil: "You know, one of the best parts of camp is that every evening after dinner, we all get together and listen to a speaker talk about God, His plan for our lives, and stories about His Son, Jesus."
Me: "Sounds good."

Then it came: the whole reason I wrote this book. Gil asked me a *simple, direct* question.

Gil: "Did you know that you could have a *personal* relationship with God?"
Me: "No?"

Gil: "Would you like that?"
I thought, *No one has ever asked me that before*, but I said,
Me: "Yeah."

Gil: "Would you like to pray with me to receive God into your heart?"
Me: "Sure."

The next thing I know, I was sitting in the very front of a bus, with kids still getting on, praying with a man that I had just met. Gil prayed a traditional prayer of salvation while I said my own but similar version, following his lead.

Us Praying

Gil: "God, we come to You, seeking to get to know You."
I said my own prayer silently following his prayer.
Me: *I don't know You and would like to.*

Gil: "We admit that we have sinned against You and that we need You to forgive us for all the unrighteous thoughts and deeds we have done in our lives."
Me: *All I know is that I've pretty much made a mess of my life so far in Your eyes, and I am sorry.*

Gil: "We ask, on the authority of Your Son, Jesus Christ, who died on the cross in our place, to forgive us of all our sins."
Me: *God, please forgive me and tell me what to do.*

Gil: "We ask that You be received in our hearts, and by Your loving grace, I ask You to save me."
Me: *If You want me the way I am, I would like nothing more than for You to take over my life from now on.*

Gil: "Amen."
Me: I just sat there silent. I was so overwhelmed by what had just happened during the prayer that I literally couldn't even say, "Amen." I had never prayed such a prayer before.

It was as if I had just presented my whole life to God in one single prayer. I not only knew that He had heard me from the bottom of my heart but something totally unexpected had also happened somewhere during this prayer. I felt as if God had actually jumped inside me. Somehow, He had landed in the very center (or soul) of my being. I felt a tremendous weight come off my shoulders and some sort of cleansing or freshness taking place. It was and still is the most incredible experience that has happened in my life.

I found out later that what I felt was God's Spirit sealing the deal that He made with anyone who prayed that prayer of salvation. At that moment, I knew that I had finally connected with the God of the universe, whom I had been seeking all my life.

The whole thing absolutely blew me away, especially by how simple it was. I finally understood why it had often been referred to as being born again. That was exactly how I felt. I felt like I was a totally new person in God's eyes. I can even distinctly remember waiting in line at the camp's store on the following day to buy something, thinking, *I'm never going to be the same again* (see 2 Corinthians 5:17).

Remember, I hadn't asked for or expected this. This was God's doing. He offers this free gift to anyone who wants to do the same thing. If you're an *anyone*, you qualify to pray this same simple prayer. This is at the heart of why I've written this book. After all the confusion of my church upbringing and searching for who and what God was, it all came down to a single one-minute prayer.

Gil: "Did you pray that prayer?"
Me: "Yes."

Gil: "How do you feel?"
Me: "Great!"

Gil: "Do you have any questions?"
Me: "Nope," I said and then thought, *Other than what just happened?*

Gil looked me in the eyes, and he could see that something had happened. Then he started to chuckle. I thought that was a little odd for just finishing such a serious prayer. Don't forget that I had just met this guy five minutes earlier. On top of that, we were still sitting in the church's parking lot. We hadn't even left for camp yet.

So I boldly said, "What's so funny?"

Gil said: "Oh Tom, I'm sorry, but you have no idea what you've just done."

I thought, *Boy, you can say that again!*

Gil continued: "I'm sorry. Let me explain. Normally when we go on these camp trips, we spend the first few days getting to know each other. We talk about things like, what is your church background? What sports or activities to you like to do? Just so we can establish a little bit about where you are in life."

"Then during the week at camp, we have many opportunities to hear and discuss things about God and His Son, Jesus, and how God's plan for us all fits together. Then on the last evening, there's what we call the Cross Talk. This is where we explain how God planned to have His Son, Jesus, come to Earth and die on the cross on our behalf to cover our sins." (I had heard this idea before in church and from Sally, but I still didn't really understand it until now.)

Gil continued, saying, "Then finally, we give everyone who has never prayed to receive His gift of salvation the opportunity to do so. And here you just did the whole thing in less than two minutes." Gil was grinning at me with what appeared to be amusement and somewhat amazement. Gil said while slightly shaking his head, "God never ceases to amaze me with His timing in our lives."

It was just like Sally talking to me and opening up a door to God. It was like my agreeing to go to camp and assuming that it would probably be another religious deal. But mainly, it was God knowing my heart and that I was more than ready to meet and finally connect with Him.

Gil sat with me the whole eight-hour trip to camp. I was trying to digest what had just happened to me when Gil opened the Bible and shared verses that explained God's plan of salvation for us. At that point, I wasn't as interested as much in how it worked as much as that it did work. Because of this unique experience for both of us, Gil and I established a lifelong bond, which few have had.

Arrived at Camp

After we got to camp, I met some of the other kids as we settled into our bunkhouse. I caught Gil telling the other counselors about me praying *the prayer* and that I had totally destroyed the camp's typical protocol by praying at the beginning instead of at the end of camp. They all seemed to have the same grin as Gil narrated this *good news* to them.

Just before we arrived at camp, Gil gave me a New Testament. I still have it. As a matter of fact, I read from it at my brother Scott's funeral in 2011. Gil came, and I told everyone the story of Gil giving it to me thirty-nine years earlier. Gil was sitting in the back with his familiar little grin, enjoying a good memory.

When he had first given it to me, I had thought, *I don't recollect ever having read anything from the Bible before.* As a matter of fact, I couldn't remember if we even had a Bible in our house. But I'm sure we did.

Gil told me to start with the Gospel of John.

I said, "Who's John, and what's a gospel?"

He chuckled, gave me that silly grin again, and said, "Here, let me show you. A gospel means good news, just like your good news of finding salvation. John was one of Jesus's followers who told us why Jesus came and what His mission on Earth was all about. It's one of four stories written about His life."

Me: "Oh, okay."

The next day at camp, I was so interested in trying to figure out what had happened to me that I didn't participate in any of the camp's morning activities. I took my New Testament, went up on the hillside all by myself, sat on a rock, and started reading the Gospel of John. I spent the whole morning devouring this book about Jesus. Everything I read was making total sense after what had happened to me the day before. I couldn't get enough. I thought, *Why didn't I read any of this before? Was any of this ever read or talked about in church and I just missed it?* I finished the whole Gospel of John in four hours that morning, just before it was time to eat lunch.

At lunch, I sat next to Gil. I asked him, "Gil, what should I read next?"

With a puzzled look on his face, Gil said, "I thought I told you to start by reading the Gospel of John?"

Me: "I did."
Gil: "What do you mean, you did?"

Me: "I finished reading the Gospel of John. What should I read next?"
Gil had a really puzzled look on his face.
Gil: "What have you been doing?"

Me: "Reading."
I explained to him about finding a rock up on the hillside where I could be alone to read and think.
Gil: "Boy, Sally told me you were special. Wow! Okay, so now I think you should read the first letter of John."

Me: "Is this the same guy that wrote the gospel I just read?"

Gil: "Yes", he said with a grin. "And Tom, see if you can fit in at least one volleyball game this afternoon."

Me: "Yeah, sure."

I almost didn't want to leave camp for fear of losing what I had. But then I realized that it wasn't about my surroundings. This new thing (salvation) was now inside and part of me. Realizing this, I was looking forward to getting home and sharing everything with my family and friends.

Back at Home

It was interesting to come home after such a life-changing experience. I can still remember being greeted by my mom, older brother, Scott, (who just graduated from high school) and my little brother, Brian, (who was age twelve and only five years younger than I was). I thought that Mom and Scott would be particularly interested in hearing about my spiritual experience. I was thinking and hoping that they might want to do the same for themselves.

Boy, was I in for a shock. I started explaining it the best way that I could about the prayer I had prayed. I told them how I felt confident that I had made a definite connection with God and that I had turned my life over to Him. They look a little confused. I continued by saying, "Yes, I have been reading the Bible about Jesus, the Son of God, and the reason that God sent Jesus to Earth to cover our sins; in order to bring us back into a right fellowship with Himself."

I thought that I had said that pretty well for being the new kid on the block. In only one week at camp, I was already grasping what had happened to me spiritually. It surprised me that I could even roughly describe what I had experienced to someone else.

Mom turned to me and said, "Well that's nice, Tom, but we are all sons and daughters in God's eyes."

I thought, *Well, this isn't going well.* I tried again, but I didn't get any further approval for my new situation. My brother Scott was looking

33

at me as if I had just joined some sort of cult. So I quit trying (see Luke 10:16).

The interesting thing was that my little brother Brian was watching and listening. I had just figured that he wouldn't be interested or even be able to understand what I was talking about, so I left him out of the conversations.

But he was watching me. Brian accepted the Lord about a year later, on his own. He told me that part of his decision to pray and ask God to save him was based on the change he saw in me. He told me that on the day I had come home from camp, I had immediately stopped teasing and picking on him. He needed to figure out the reason why. He wanted what I had. I was the first person that he told after he had prayed his own prayer of salvation.

That is how it works. I saw and heard something from Sally. Brian saw and heard something from me. Our mom heard Brian give his testimony in front of the whole church one Sunday and decided that she had seen and heard enough from her two boys to be able to do the same. Independent of us, Scott also came home on a college break and announced his decision.

That September, I started my senior year in high school. I arrived as a different person than I had been the previous year. I can distinctly remember that before my conversion, I had always tried so hard to get people to like me and think that I was a pretty cool guy. Well now, I really didn't care about any of that. I had the God of the universe inside me. How much more important could I feel? What more could anyone else offer me? My personal search for total acceptance had been met (Do you remember back in the Introduction, my asking, "Do you feel like you're important?").

Now my mission was to tell and help others find what I had found. I realized quite often that I wasn't very good at explaining it. The problem was that I was explaining a non-tangible idea. It was a spiritual matter that dealt with the heart and a need to connect with God. But that didn't stop me from trying.

The second problem I had was that most of

the kids I talked to in school informed me that they already had their own religion and that they didn't need a new one. I received answers like, "I'm already a Christian, and I go to church." Some of my close Jewish friends let me know that their families would never allow them to go and listen to a message about Jesus or any of that being saved stuff.

Wow, I was getting a reality check regarding my newly found spiritual life and trying to share it with others. It was interesting that most of the kids I talked to felt threatened at the idea of attending a Christian activity outside of what they were used to, especially when it had to do with their parents. But they would spend lunchtime and after-school hours listening to my story. They asked me questions about how it related to where they were in their thoughts about God. Sometimes they would question the religious beliefs and ideas that they had grown up with, as I had.

I saw many kids accept God's plan of salvation through my efforts. I realized that God was the one who always drew them in and sealed the deal. It was and still is a mystery to me how God does this and works in people's lives. I still enjoy sitting back and hearing someone say, "I did it," meaning that they prayed the prayer of salvation and God freely and graciously answered them.

It's always interesting to look back on your senior year. Do you remember that you mostly knew the kids who were in your class? You also may have known a few in the class above or below you.

Without even thinking about it and as I tried to talk to as many kids as I could, by the end of my senior year, I must have known five-to-ten kids in every homeroom and in every class level. I was actually accused by one of my close senior classmates of running a popularity contest for myself. That struck me as a very interesting view of what was really going on. But as I saw some kids come to know the Lord through my efforts, it more than made up for all the criticism that may have been falsely thrown my way.

One time, a freshman boy's mom arrived

to pick him up after a Young Life meeting. She profusely thanked me for helping him. She said, "I don't know what you did or told him, but he's not the same insecure kid and is so happy now."

I said, "I just pointed him in the same direction that I took. God was the one who changed him."

That was my start. From the beginning of this new life, I was amazed at the people who listened to me, who wanted it for themselves, and who weren't at all interested. God is the only one who really knows our hearts. As an example, I can think of a least five people whom I did not share God's plan of salvation with because I knew that I would be wasting my time. I saw their selfish attitudes and the things that they were doing and thought, *They would be the last people on Earth that would listen to or even care about any of this.*

I was wrong. At some point in their lives, someone shared the story of salvation with them, and each of these five people did the same thing that I had done. They asked God to come in and take over. When they told me about their experience, I apologized for not sharing it with them. They each told me, "Oh, that's okay. I was a pretty messed up person back then, and I may not have listened to you anyway. But God finally got a hold of me when I was ready."

To this day, I'm still amazed that when someone prays to be saved, it always works. I shouldn't doubt that it will work, but we're dealing with something that is nothing less than miraculous. It can't be explained in a physical way. You just have to try it and see for yourself. Are you ready?

Reference Verses

Therefore if anyone is in Christ, he is a new creation; the old things passed away; behold, new things have come. (2 Corinthians 5:17 NKJV)

He who hears you, hears Me, he who rejects you rejects Me. And he who rejects Me rejects Him who sent Me. (Luke 10:16 NKJV)

MY CHALLENGE

Reflecting back to 1972 when I said the prayer of salvation, I realize how simple it was. I've always been intrigued by how complex everyone has made it. I have always emphasized its simplicity when sharing my story. So I finally decided to come up with a way to express it, by writing a book that I hope will simplify and explain it all. I wanted to come up with a formula, as an experiment, that had a simple step-by-step process that anyone could follow.

It does not matter where you are in life, what religious background you have, or even where you think you stand with God. My challenge is this: I want you to get through this entire book and see for yourself if salvation is real or not. Why don't you spend some time checking it out without pressure from others? Yes, it's a challenge. Can you get through this entire experiment, fill in all the ingredients as suggested, and possibly find the same results that so many of us have found in the past? Before we start the experiment, let's look at the meaning of the book's title.

"A Final Experiment"

A

This word means *one* or a *single* item. There are many different ways to present the message of God's plan of salvation. This *one* is mine. It is my unique story of how I came to connect with God. I'm also using the word *A* in the title because it may be the one and only time you ever consider looking at this thing called salvation.

Final

Why don't you *finally* take a hard look at this topic and decide for yourself if it works. Decide if it's true or if it's just another man-made religious concept. Maybe you think that you are secure in your relationship with God because of your religious upbringing. Maybe this experiment will double-check or confirm that thought. On the other hand, maybe you're sick and tired of hearing all this Jesus saves stuff, and you would like to have it presented to you from an average guy who stumbled upon it one day.

There have been countless numbers of people over the centuries who have spent much time trying to disprove Christianity as the only way to God, only to finally discover the overwhelming evidence that has led them to a relationship with Him. If you are on either end of this spectrum, my challenge to you is to take some time and *finally* decide for yourself.

Experiment

An experiment is a process or procedure that is repeated many times to substantiate whether a hypothesis is valid or not. An experiment that is repeated to test a theory will eventually prove or disprove it. In this case, I am going to present a formula, which if done correctly will result in you connecting with and having a direct, personal relationship with God. My challenge for you is to perform this entire experiment, add all the necessary ingredients, and let me know the results.

Let's also look at the subtitle:

"A Simple, Direct and Personal Formula to Connect with God."

Simple

This word is the main reason that I wrote this book. In the forty plus years since my conversion, my story of salvation that you just read, I have heard of very few people who have accepted God's gift of grace (salvation) in an easier, quicker, or *simpler* way than I have.

I find it interesting that God meant for His plan of salvation to be simple. I see that humans and religion have complicated it. There are no rituals, ceremonies, or special words needed. Either you desire a real relationship with God or you don't. Maybe so far, you've gone through life thinking that you have arrived because you've done everything your religious leaders have told you to do. In other words, you've worked for your salvation. It doesn't work that way. As a matter of fact, if you look back on the prayer that I said with Gil, my thoughts were worded differently than his. God was listening to my heart. My prayer was simple and untraditional, but God knew what I meant and answered me.

Bringing yourself to ask God to save you may be one of the hardest things your mind will have to do. But it's actually one of the easiest things to do once you're ready. It's that simple.

Direct

This is an important part of the formula. The whole idea of salvation happens between you and God. You cannot be saved because someone else tells you that you are. I don't want to cause any conflicts, and I don't know how you were brought up or what you've been told. But you have to make a direct connection with God and not do it through any religious ritual or leader. You'll start to see this as you go through the experiment.

Personal

Remember Gil asking me, "Did you know that you could have a *personal* relationship with God? What a *simple* and *direct* question. *Personal* has always meant deep down inside, intimate, or very close. I used to think that God stayed where He was in a place like heaven or at an arm's length—where you knew He was around or felt He was close by. I found out that He wanted to come in and live (His Spirit) inside me. You can't get much more personal than that.

Formula

What would an experiment be without a formula? A formula contains *ingredients* and has a *process* for adding or mixing these ingredients so that you come up with a specific result. You can think of it as a recipe. The ingredients have to be combined in a specific way. You have to do each step in a specific order. If you don't, it won't work.

I use this idea in this book. I will present all the key ingredients: attitudes, ideas, and spiritual conditions. You must place these one at a time in your experimental "spiritual beaker". You will combine them in a final *simple* prayer, which will result in a *direct, personal,* and permanent connection with God. If it doesn't work, you left something out. If it does work, well, welcome to the club.

Connect

Connect means "to become joined" (Webster). *Joined* is the key word. There is a whole section where I explain the difference between *feeling*

God and *knowing* God. This direct and personal connection is real. Just like a lamp with a cord, you have to plug it in to connect with a source so that it will work. In other words, when you make a solid connection, you will experience a spiritual power force, God's Spirit plugged into yours. Right now, you're either on or off. Don't worry; this experiment will get you connected.

THE EXPERIMENT

A FEW GENERAL OBSERVATIONS, DISCLAIMERS, AND GROUND RULES BEFORE WE START THE EXPERIMENT

Who Am I Writing To?

First of all, I'm writing to people like me, who grew up in a church but were never clear on the salvation topic. Most traditional churches, Catholic or Protestant, assume that you are going to heaven because you were baptized as an infant. We always heard and repeated prayers stating that Jesus was the Son of God and died on the cross to save us from our sins. But did we really understand or believe either of these ideas deep down inside? Were they even true? As you just read in my story, I found out that there is a *time of salvation*, a specific one-time prayer when you sincerely ask God to save you.

To all my Jewish friends, I know that you have been taught that an earthly Messiah is to come. Most Jews do not know that all their Old Testament prophecies speak of Jesus's birth, genealogy, teachings, death, and resurrection in detail. He did come. He was a Jew. Where do you think Christians came from? No offense, but He was the Messiah. Don't dismiss this idea until you get through this experiment. Some of my favorite stories are from Jewish people who realized that Jesus was who He said He was and accepted Him as their Messiah or Savior. Yes, many of them have been ostracized by their families for going against their families' traditions (see John 5:46–47 and Acts 13:39).

For anyone who is following another religion, I do not have the time in this book to compare my beliefs to yours. I have over many years examined almost every spiritual or religious idea that is out there, to find none that offers me a personal and direct connection with God. To those of you who consider yourselves agnostics or atheists, I address this in the First Ingredient. Please try this experiment and see if there may be something better in store for you than what you currently believe or think, or ideology that you might be following.

I Refer to God as "He"

I am not a male chauvinist, but the Bible speaks of God as a loving and good Father. So I will also. I hope this doesn't stop you from doing the experiment.

Quoting the Bible

I am going to present verses from the Bible (in parentheses) as I go. I will quote them at the end of each chapter so that you can refer to them if you want to. I am not going to assume that you believe the Bible is God-inspired versus man-written. Personally, I had never read anything in the Bible before I prayed my initial prayer of salvation. I tell people, "I didn't know an epistle from an apostle." I am not even sure we had a Bible in our house growing up. Many verses in the Bible, even if taken at face value, say much about each ingredient in the experiment, so please read them.

I Am Not a Salesman

I am not going to try to sell you on any of this. I'm not going to argue, debate, or try to persuade you in any way. This is all for you to decide. The whole idea of salvation is between you and God. Do you remember *direct* and *personal* in the subtitle? However, you must consider your life after your death. This issue of *salvation* may be an important one between you and God when you meet Him face to face someday.

The last thing that I want is for you to be exactly like me, other than accepting God's plan of salvation. I don't want you to look like me, dress like me, or even go to the same church as me. God has made you, you. You are a unique person that

He wants to have a personal relationship with. The only pushy thing that I'm going to do is challenge you to do this experiment and see if it works.

My Credentials

I do not have a PhD from a theological seminary. However, I do have a post hole digger (PHD) that I keep in the back of my pickup. I'm just letting you know that I am an average guy sharing my personal story, thoughts, and ideas about the most important thing that has happened in my life.

Take a "Time-Out"

Before we start the experiment, let's talk about taking "time-outs". This will be a very valuable tool as you go through the experiment. It's not only a suggestion, but I think you will find it essential in sorting out whether you should continue or not.

So here's what you do. Whenever you feel that you need it, stop for a time-out. Pray to God and ask Him if what you have just read is what He wants you to know or do. Each part of this experiment is going to challenge you to place an important spiritual ingredient into your so-called spiritual beaker. You don't need to do it because I suggested it. Ask God if it's what He wants you to do and if you should continue with the experiment.

Remember, God listens to your heart and not your thoughts (see "H.O.W." below). If you stop, take a time-out to pray, God will answer you. How does He do this? If you will be still and quiet, God's Spirit, who is a small, calm voice that talks to you through your inner sprit, will let you know that this is what He wants you to do.

Maybe you've never tried this before. Well, that's good. It may be a whole new start for you. Please don't think it's all some sort of psychosomatic trick. If you're sincerely seeking God, He will draw near to you (see James 4:8). That's how He works. He will never bang your door down, and you will not ever hear an audible voice. You should feel Him saying, "This is okay," "Keep going," "I'm here with you," or, "This is what I desire for you."

Stop, take a time-out, and pray as much and as often as you need to. If you do this throughout the experiment, you should wind up with a new perspective on prayer and begin a new personal and direct relationship with God, maybe for the first time in your life (James 1:5). Next, I'll show you H.O.W. you should pray.

H.O.W. (Honesty, Open-Minded, and Willingness)

I am borrowing concept from many well-known self-help groups that use it as a tool. I am slightly revising the usage of each item to fit our purposes.

Honesty (H)

This exercise is to show you how God listens to our prayers. Okay, so I'm going to ask you a question. See if you can answer it *honestly*. "If you died today, would you go to heaven?"

A) I don't know.
B) I think so. At least that's what I've been told by my church, family, or others.
C) I've been baptized, confirmed, or had a bar mitzvah, so I guess I'm good to go.
D) I hope so, but I'm not sure.

For example, if you can't remember a time in your life that you prayed a specific prayer of salvation, your *honest* answer would either be A or D. These answers are honest because they are from the heart. If you answered B or C, you have stored these answers in your head, and they are not from your heart. Others have told you (head knowledge) that you're okay, but do you honestly believe that you are?

Let's see how honesty works with God, specifically, regarding how we pray to God. There are three types of prayers. Two of them are self-driven and one is God-driven.

Pray Aloud (Self-Driven)

We pray aloud when we're in a group or with our family, usually at the dinner table. Of course, we assume that God hears our words. But how sincere are we when we are talking to or asking for something from Him? Are we just impressing others with our prayer? Doesn't God know if we're sincere or not?

Pray Silently (Self-Driven)

We usually pray this type of prayer when we're alone. We hope that God will hear this prayer through our thoughts. Again, are we sincere? Are we thinking that God only hears our thoughts and not our hearts?

A Prayer from the Heart (God-Driven)

Whether we are actually praying or not, if God is who He says He is, He already knows the true natures, motives, and intentions of our hearts. God looks beyond our words or thoughts and sees what's *honestly* going on inside us. In other words, we can't fool God. He knows us better than we know ourselves (see Jeremiah 29:13).

The bottom line is that if you cannot be honest with yourself and God, this experiment will not work for you. Otherwise, let's start thinking and praying honestly and see what happens.

Open-Minded (O)

Many people think of born-again Christians as Bible-thumping, close-minded people. On the surface, I can understand this view. However, I would suggest that in order for you to accept this salvation concept, you have to be very *open-minded*. Let me try to explain from two common views.

1) A Democratic View

On the surface, this view seems to be very open-minded. It suggests that no single religion is absolutely the right one. Each person has his or her own pathway to God and receives some value when pursuing their own spiritual avenue.

2) There's Only One True Religion View

Hypothetically speaking, consider this: What if there was only *one* true religion? Wouldn't that make everything simpler and easier for us? The problem is that you would have to be very open-minded, to accept such a simple concept, right? Well, that's what I am suggesting in this book. Do you think you can keep an open mind? You will need this capability throughout this experiment. So give it a shot and ask God to help you keep an open mind to what He may open your eyes to. (Matthew 7:13–14 & John 4:16)

Willingness (W)

Willingness is the ability to try something for which you do not know the end results.

This is a perfect word for this book. You may be navigating in several uncharted spiritual waters during this experiment. You will need to be willing to try each step as we go through them.

A biblical term for willingness is faith. Faith is believing in things unseen, and there are lots of these in this experiment. You must be willing to be honest and open as you place each ingredient into your spiritual beaker. You must also have faith that a prayer of salvation will connect you to a direct and personal relationship with God.

Please use these H.O.W. principles in your time-out prayers as needed throughout this experiment. Remember, this is an experiment. The ingredients have to be added in their proper order. The following chapters will explain each ingredient and the order in which it should be added. The final result will add up to you finding a simple, direct, and personal connection with God.

Please note that none of these steps can be skipped. Each ingredient has to be considered, accepted, and added to your spiritual beaker. Remember to take time-outs and to pray as you consider each one.

If for any reason you cannot accept an ingredient, please make sure that you read the last chapter, "I'll Take My Chances," before putting the book down.

Here is a picture of your complete

"Spiritual Beaker"

Ingredients

Expect a Result
God Will Let You Know That He Has Done This

5

Ask God to Save You
Ask Him to Forgive You, Clean House, Come into Your Life, and Take Over

4

Admit Your Sinful Nature
I've Ignored God and Live a Self-Centered Life

3

Express Your Need for God
I Wish to Have a Real Relationship with God

2

Acknowledge God
Allow God to Reveal Himself

1

Reference Verses

[Jesus said] If you believed Moses, you would believe Me, for he wrote about Me. But if you do not believe his writings, how will you believe My words? (John 5:46–47 NKJV)

Draw near to God and He will draw near to you. (James 4:8 NKJV)

Through him everyone who believes is set free from every sin, a justification you were not able to obtain under the law of Moses. (Acts 13:39 NIV)

If any of you lacks wisdom, you should ask God, who gives generously without finding fault, and it will be given you. (James 1:5 NIV)

You will seek Me and find Me when you search for Me with all your heart. (Jeremiah 29:13 NKJV)

Enter through the narrow gate. For wide is the gate and broad is the road that leads to destruction, and many enter through it. But small is the gate and narrow the road that leads to life, and only a few find it. (Matthew 7:13–14 NIV)

Jesus said to him: I am the way, the truth, and the life. No one comes to the Father except through me. (John 14:6 NKJV)

Salvation is found in no one else, for there is no other name under heaven given to mankind by which we must be saved. (Acts 4:12 NIV)

FIRST INGREDIENT

ACKNOWLEDGE GOD
Allow God to Reveal Himself

I mentioned that I wasn't going to quote many Bible verses unless they were useful as a general reference. But it's interesting that the first four words in the Bible are, "In the beginning, God" (Genesis 1:1 NKJV).

Salvation Beaker

Acknowledge God

This is also where we need to begin.

Is there a God? If you can't at least acknowledge God's existence, you cannot move into a relationship with Him. Who He is will be an ongoing revelation after you have connected with Him. I believe every one of us falls into one of the following three categories.

Atheist: Does Not Believe God Exists

From my experience, these people do not feel that there is any real evidence that God exists. They feel that God and religion are man-made institutions and ideas that were made to help explain our existence here on Earth. They also think that these made-up beliefs help satisfy our need to know who we are, how we got here, and what our purpose is while we are here. An atheist's basic philosophy is, "If God can't be easily found, physically located, or measured in a scientific way, there is no proof that He exists."

Although, I find it interesting that I also hear comments from atheists that go something like this: "I don't really think there is a God or anything that's in charge of this whole universe. But on the other hand, I'm sad to think that when I die, that's it! We die, we get buried, worms get a free meal, and there is nothing more for us."

Part of an atheists' outlook is not being able to see a *spiritual* part of their lives (see John 4:24). Everything has to be seen, heard, or touched to be real. On the surface, this makes sense. If you think about it, it demands God to reveal Himself physically to us. Maybe, just maybe, that's why God sent Jesus to Earth, but that's down the road in another chapter. Atheists seek *head* knowledge of God because they will only believe if they can physically experience Him.

Instead, God is looking for a *heart* relationship with you. Even though we can't explain exactly where it is, most of us feel that there is a place deep within us that we call our soul. Sometimes, it is referred to as the very core of our being. I would like to suggest that this inner part was made and reserved for one purpose: God's Spirit. God's

Spirit is the only thing that can fill it. Maybe you have been trying all your life to fill it with other things or ideas that you thought would satisfy this void, but they haven't. Maybe you should try to fill it with God.

How do you do this? In the preceding chapter, I addressed this topic called H.O.W. (Honesty, Open-Minded, and Willingness). You can reread it now if that will help you. Or take a time-out and ask God to *reveal* Himself to you, maybe for the first time in your life. Then you can honestly *acknowledge* that He does exist (see John 5:40).

Agnostic: Not Sure If There Is a God or Not

This person is not sure if there is a God or not. On the one hand, it would make perfect sense for there to be a mastermind behind this whole universe—someone or something that set it in motion and that is still in charge.

On the other hand, you still have many questions. There are certain things that you need to know before you can *acknowledge* God's existence or accept His authority in your life. Here is a short list of some of those unanswered topics:

dinosaurs, fossils, diseases, human suffering, UFOs, aliens, evolution, life on other planets, the Big Bang theory, ghosts, the Loch Ness Monster, Big Foot, controversial social issues, other religious beliefs

Did I miss something else that you must have an answer to before you can believe in God's existence?

If you cannot look into God's existence until you have a satisfactory answer to one or more of these topics, think about this: the chances are that you will die before you get any kind of satisfactory answer to any of these. The point is, you're stuck on something that may or may not matter in the long run.

I am a believer in God's existence. I have a connection with Him through my prayer of salvation, and I still can't answer most of these questions. What you will get on the other side of this salvation experience is a comfort that God knows the answers. These topics don't have anything to do with having a relationship with Him. You won't care if any of these topics are answered. You will have many new questions about heaven and life after death, which *will be* answered.

I think most agnostics have this position: "I'm not against there being a God. But if He exists, I will allow Him to reveal Himself to me." That's interesting. You will allow Him? Aren't you trying to play God? So is He God or are you God? I think this might be a key point in your being able to move aside your demands to have answers and allow Him to do things His way for you, and see what happens. God cannot be in charge if you are.

This may be a good place for a time-out and for you to work the H.O.W. into your prayer. Ask God to reveal Himself in your heart and let you know He's there cheering you on.

I Believe There Is a God

This is the first ingredient we need to put into our Salvation Beaker. It is a very necessary basic part of this formula, even if our ideas of God are different. Some of us may see Him as a *Higher Power* or the *Supreme Force* that runs the universe. It's only important for you to *acknowledge* that He exists so that you can begin this experiment. It does not matter what your religious background is or which church, synagogue, or temple you've come from. The important thing is that you believe God is there, whether you understand how it all works or not.

Okay, here's the second part of acknowledging God's existence. Maybe it has always made sense that some *Higher Power* started everything and is in charge. But if you take it a step further, you need to ask Him to reveal Himself.

Allow God to Reveal
Himself to You

Believing in God is still only head knowledge. We need to ask God to *reveal* Himself to our hearts. You should take a time-out and apply a H.O.W. prayer now. Open yourself up (*open-minded*) and pray *honestly* from your heart for God to reveal Himself to you. Be *willing* to allow Him to draw near to you, as He promises He will (see James 4:8). If your prayer is sincere, you will feel His Spirit touching yours and your relationship with Him starting to click. Go ahead and try it.

Can you put the First Ingredient into your Spiritual Beaker? If you can, that's great. We can go to the Second Ingredient. If you are still contemplating God's existence, you have two choices.

Option 1) Stay on this chapter as you take some time to seek God through prayer, to wait for Him to let you know He's there, and to tell Him that you desire to begin a new relationship with Him.

Option 2) You'll have to work out, on your own, your unanswered questions, resentments, or reasons why you can't Acknowledge God's Existence. Please make sure you read the last chapter "I'll Take My Chances" before closing this book.

Reference Verses

God is Spirit, and those who worship Him must worship in spirit and truth. (John 4:24 NKJV)

But you are not willing to come to Me that you may have life. (John 5:40 NKJV)

Draw near to God, and He will draw near to you. (James 4:8 NKJV)

SECOND INGREDIENT

EXPRESS YOUR NEED
FOR GOD
I Wish to Have a Real Relationship
with God

Hopefully, you were able to honestly acknowledge the existence of God and place this as the first ingredient into your Salvation Beaker. For this second ingredient, we must consider

Salvation Beaker

Express Your Need for God

Acknowledge God

whether we need or want a real and personal relationship with God. Let me give you three specific reasons that illustrate why we should need a real relationship with God.

1) The Key

I'm sure many of you come from the same religious background that I do. We went to our places of worship and did everything we were told to do so that we could be in right standing with God. If you were like me, you hoped that it was enough for God's approval. I always thought I was pretending that it was all good, but deep down inside, I felt that it was somewhat shallow.

As you read in "My Story," I found that the key was a specific prayer that really started my spiritual journey. Let me give you a quick analogy to illustrate this. When I was seven or eight years old, my best friend, Steve, and I would play this game: We'd sneak into my mom's car and pretend that we were going on a road trip. We had a blast mimicking our parents.

First, we put our pretend kids in the back seat and made them put on their imaginary seat belts—no wives, just kids. It was an interesting concept. It was just me, Steve, and our kids (Girls had cooties back then). Next, we adjusted the mirrors, put on our seat belts, pretended to turn on the radio and then started the car with imaginary keys. Now we were off on our vacation. We would play out the whole trip, including stopping for gas. Occasionally, we had to turn around and yell at our pretend kids, "Pipe down," or, "Keep your hands to yourselves."

This was all for fun. It was interesting that we were in a real car, but we could not go anywhere because we didn't have the real keys to start the car. So, let's relate this story to our church experience (or your place of worship).

1) We were sitting in a Christian church, therefore, we must have been Christians and going to heaven. Steve and I were

sitting in a car, so we must have been going somewhere.

2) We went to church regularly and did all the things that we were supposed to do to secure our place in God's kingdom. Steve and I did everything to get ready for our trip. We put our seat belts on and adjusted everything. We were ready to go. We couldn't really go anywhere because we didn't have the real keys.

We think that we are going somewhere by attending church and doing what we are told, but if we don't start our spiritual relationship with God by saying a specific prayer of salvation, we are still in park. The key to connecting with God and starting a real relationship with Him is through the prayer of salvation. You need to have the *key*.

2) Feeling vs. Knowing God

God wants to have a real and permanent relationship with us. That is why He made us with a spiritual receptor and transmitter, which we typically refer to as our soul. He is not going to push Himself on us. He is waiting for us to come to Him when we are ready and willing.

You may say, "Throughout the years, I have felt God after praying to Him", and you have. God wants you to seek Him. The feeling is real, but it's only a *feeling* of God's presence. Wouldn't you like to take this to the next level and get to *know* God personally?

Right now, you're still at an arm's length from God. You pray to God when you need something or want to thank Him for something. He hears you and responds. But you have not expressed your need to know Him personally. I don't mean only relating to Him through prayer occasionally but letting Him know that you want Him to come inside you and take over. This is what He's really waiting for you to do.

Here's the closest analogy that I can think of. We have all had feelings for someone whom we wanted to know better or fell in love with. This was a great feeling, right? But you didn't really know that person until he or she became your intimate partner. This form of intimacy is very similar to God's desire to have a relationship with us. He wants a definite connection, an intimate relationship, not just to be an acquaintance.

Here's one of the main reasons that you may want to express a need to know God. One day, we're all going to die. According to most religions, we are going to face God and answer for our lives. What if God looks at you and says, "Who are you?" "Do I know you?" Of course, these are rhetorical questions. He knows who you are. What He's saying is that you and He never really got to know each other at a specific time when you prayed for Him to come into your life. You never really connected in a permanent way.

3) Insurance vs. Assurance

Insurance

We are all very familiar with the need for insurance. It seems like every part of our lives requires us to invest in an insurance policy. It is designed to protect us against a future catastrophic event, which could disrupt or ruin our lives, physically or financially.

Insurance is a simple idea.

1) We invest a small amount of money that will guarantee our protection in case of an unforeseen event in the future.
2) We weigh our investment premiums against the benefits that it might produce.
3) Of course, some of us will take our chances, and we will not have insurance at all. Someday, we might regret our decision.

This insurance concept parallels with the need to insure your eternal life with God. So let's change one of our life insurance policies into one of God's life assurance policies.

Assurance

Does God offer a life insurance policy? Yes, it's called an eternal life assurance policy. His policy offers you a guaranteed and secure eternal life. Unlike having to keep working to pay for the premiums on an insurance policy, God's assurance policy is a one-time deal. You ask God to approve your request for this assurance policy. Not only does He accept it but you also don't have to pay Him for it; it's free. In reality, God paid it for you through Jesus (but that chapter is still coming).

Let's compare these two ideas:

1) Insurance: We invest a small amount of money that will guarantee our protection in the case of an event in the future.

   Assurance: We invest a small amount of time from our lives (as you're doing right now by reading this book) that will lead to guaranteeing our eternal future.

2) Insurance: We weigh the investment premiums and compare them with the potential benefits.
Assurance: With one simple prayer (investment), God promises us eternal life with Him.

3) Insurance: Some will take their chances without insurance and someday regret that decision.
Assurance: You may be thinking that you don't need this salvation experience. You're also hoping that someday (after death), you won't regret this decision.

You either are investing the time to look into it now or are going to take your chances and hope that nothing bad happens to you because of your decision.

Express Your Need for God

Let's review the Second Ingredient.

> **The Key:** Quit pretending that you're okay with God. The *key* is a one-time prayer of salvation.

> **Know God:** Quit only feeling God's presence and get to *know* Him personally.

> **Assurance:** Quit taking risks with your eternity. Your *assurance* policy is God's free gift.

I hope these three examples have helped you express your need to obtain a direct, personal, and permanent relationship with God. If so, check off the Second Ingredient and place it in your Spiritual Beaker.

Remember, if you need a time-out to ask God if He wants you to keep going, do so. Use the H.O.W. principles in your prayer. Don't rush any of these steps. You honestly need to want to do each one. If you can't put this Second Ingredient in, please make sure that you read the last chapter "I'll Take My Chances" before closing the book.

Reference Verses

I will give you the keys of the kingdom of heaven. (Matthew 16:19 NIV)

For what profit is it to a man if he gains the whole world, and loses his own soul? Or what will a man give in exchange for his soul? (Matthew 16:26 NKJV)

But He will say, "I tell you, I do not know you or where you're from. Get away from Me, all you evildoers!" (Luke 13:27 CSB)

Let us draw near to God with a sincere heart and with the full assurance that faith brings, having our hearts sprinkled to cleanse us from a guilty conscience and having our bodies washed with pure water. (Hebrews 10:22 NIV)

THIRD INGREDIENT

ADMIT YOUR SINFUL NATURE
I've Ignored God and Live a Self-Centered Life

Hopefully, you have been able to Acknowledge God's Existence (1st Ingredient) and you have established the Need to Know Him (2nd Ingredient). Hopefully, you have successfully and honestly put then into your Spiritual Beaker.

Salvation Beaker

Admit Your Sinful Nature

Express Your Need for God

Acknowledge God

This next step may be the hardest thing to add to your beaker, but you've come this far by being honest, open-minded, and willing (H.O.W.), so let's look at our sin nature.

What Is Sin?

Most people define sin as breaking one of the Ten Commandments, which are found in Exodus 20:2–17 and Deuteronomy 5:6–21 (NKJV).

1) You shall have no other gods before me.
2) You shall make no idols (paraphrased).
3) You shall not take the name of the Lord your God in vain.
4) Remember the Sabbath day, keep it holy.
5) Honor your Father and your Mother.
6) You shall not murder.
7) You shall not commit adultery.
8) You shall not steal.
9) You shall not bear false witness against your neighbor.
10) You shall not covet (your neighbor's house).

These sins can be the actions that are described here or even the thoughts of doing them (see Matthew 5:27–28). God knows our thoughts, motives, and intentions, even if we think He only sees our actions (see Matthew 15:19). So looking down the list, we have done some of these or at least thought about doing many of them.

You might be thinking, *Well, nobody's perfect!* You're right. This brings me to our first topic.

Nobody's Perfect

This is not only something we all can agree with, but God knows that we can never achieve it. However, He wants us to be perfect. In other words, He sees what we would be like if we were perfect in His eyes. This is what He desires for us. He sees what we would be like if we hadn't done certain things, thought bad things, or been self-centered most of the time. We can't go back and undo what we've already done. So what's God's plan to fix all this? Let's focus on the problem of sin first, and then we'll start fixing it in the next chapter (see Romans 3:23).

What Is Sin?

My Simplified Definition

I have often had problems defining what sin is when talking to people about God's plan for their lives. Is it only about actions or bad thoughts? Is it about how many we've done or how often we do them? People have these questions about sin.

I have narrowed sin down to one word: "Ignore". Think about it. If God desires a personal, intimate, and perfect relationship with us, we should be thinking about Him 24/7, right? It's impossible, right? My simplified (my favorite thing to do) definition of sin is that we have ignored God and the things that He wants for us. This includes not having a real connection with Him and not accepting His plan of salvation. The amount of time that we have ignored Him isn't important, whether it's years, months, days, or hours.

The main point is that our sinful nature causes a self-centered attitude. Our focus is on ourselves while we ignore Him. I hope this makes sense. This brings me to my next point in admitting our sinful nature (see Proverbs 28:13 and 1 John 1:8).

Justification

We agree that none of us is perfect. Okay, but what if we're not that bad? Now we're talking about justifying our actions and thoughts. Maybe you know you have sinned big-time. Or maybe you don't feel that any of your sins are all that "big a deal".

Whether we've realized it or not, we all have a justification defense ready to present if we have to answer to God when we die. I'm sure you have heard of people who have had life-threatening experiences. They tell us that their whole lives flashed before their eyes in detail. Maybe this is evidence that God will show us the sinful nature that we've had throughout our lives. We'll see every selfish action, thought, and motive that we did or had during our time on Earth.

Here is a list of some typical justifications that many of us are prepared to use.

1) Good versus Bad: I think that overall, my good things will outweigh the bad things that I have done.

2) Good Works: I have done so many good things for others throughout my life.

3) Best I Could Do: I've done the best I could with what I was given.

4) Religious: I always went to church, mass, temple, and Bible studies and prayed daily. What more could I have done?

5) Comparison: This one's a biggie for many of us.
   A) Compared to most people I know, I'm a pretty good person.
   B) I'm better than some of those hypocritical born-again Christians that I've seen.

6) God Is Love: If God claims that He loves us, He should let us all into heaven, right?

7) Sin of Omission: I've kept to myself, taken care of my family, and haven't bothered anyone (Okay, but have you seen others in need and ignored them? This is the deceptive sin of self-centeredness).

8) Defiant: If God doesn't want me the way I am, then fine, I don't want to be with Him either.

Do you have one or more of these justifications ready to give? Well, let me tell you a few things that you need to think about. These things may help you see and admit your sinful nature.

1) God desires you to be perfect. He knows you're not. If you can admit you have a sinful nature, He has a plan to restore you to the perfect place that He sees for you.

2) You will be on your own in front of Him someday. You will not be able to have an attorney present.

3) You do not get a second chance once you die. God will ask, "Why didn't you receive my free gift of forgiveness and restitution for all your sins when you had the chance?"

You may be thinking, *But I always thought God was fair.*

Fair vs. Just

Our human idea of God being fair when judging us means that He would consider the good we've done versus the bad or even how good we've been compared to others. But what if God dealt with each one of us individually, as if we were the only person who ever lived on Earth? There is no one else to compare your good and bad with. Are you good enough? Wasn't God expecting you to be perfect? But you're not. Because you wanted your own way. You were self-serving. In other words, ignored Him. Therefore, wouldn't any judgement He authorized because of your faults be just?

Someday, it's going to be just you and God, face-to-face. Are you ready to admit your sinful nature to Him? Have you been ignoring God and His plan to restore you to a true relationship with Him? If you are, go ahead and add the Third Ingredient to your Salvation Beaker.

If you are still struggling with the sin-nature topic and can't honestly add it, why don't you take a time-out and use your H.O.W. tool? Pray sincerely for God to reveal some of the past sins that you have committed. Use this time to allow Him to remind you that He is there and that He wants to restore and forgive you. He just wants you to admit that you have ignored Him so that you can continue this experiment and finally get His gift of salvation, which has been promised to you. If you can't honestly admit your sinful nature and plan to stop here, please make sure you read the last chapter "I'll Take My Chances" before closing this book.

Reference Verses

You have heard that it was said, "You shall not commit adultery." But I tell you that anyone who looks at a woman lustfully has already committed adultery with her in his heart. (Matthew 5:27-28 NIV)

For out of the heart come evil thoughts—murder, adultery, sexual immorality, theft, false testimony, slander. (Matthew 15:19 NIV)

For all have sinned and fall short of the glory of God. (Romans 3:23 NKJV)

Whoever conceals the sins does not prosper, but who confesses and renounces the finds mercy. (Proverbs 28:13 NIV)

If we say that we have no sin, we deceive ourselves, and the truth is not in us. (1 John 1:8 NKJV)

The Lord our God is merciful and forgiving, even though we have rebelled against Him. (Daniel 9:9 NIV)

FOURTH INGREDIENT
ASK GOD TO SAVE YOU
Ask Him to Forgive You, Clean House, Come into Your Life, and Take Over

If you have come this far and have added the first three ingredients with an honest, open, and a willing heart (H.O.W.), you are ready to add the forth ingredient. When you put all

Salvation Beaker

Ask God to Save You

Admit Your Sinful Nature

Express Your Need for God

Acknowledge God

four of these together, you will be ready to start a real and permanent relationship with God by asking God to save you through a prayer of salvation.

Some people call this a time of salvation because it may be the first time in your life that you have asked God to forgive you of your sins and to restore you to His perfect image for you. Some might think that they have already done this at some time in their lives. If you are not sure, let's make sure. Either way, God wants to give you the assurance policy that He is offering.

How Does the Prayer Work?

I can tell you what to pray. We're going to do that in this chapter. I can't tell you exactly how it works. I just know that if you pray a sincere prayer, God hears your heart. He hears you asking for forgiveness and for Him to come in and save you. I have asked many people who are born-again Christians, and they say the same thing:

"We're not sure how it works. We just know that it does" (see Proverbs 3:5).

You may think that is a weak answer, but it is a hidden treasure from God (Ephesians 3:9). No one will ever be able to physically or mentally find it. It can only be obtained when your spirit finds His. When you get on the other side of your salvation experience, you will know that it happened to you, but you will not be able to explain how it happened. God will give you assurance that you have connected with Him through your prayer of salvation. His Spirit will enter you, in that God shaped void inside you, for the first time to seal the deal.

If you remember back in "My Story," I expressed that I felt God's Spirit, which was an unexpected result of me knowing that God and I had connected. That's how we know that God has heard us and saved us. You will know without a doubt that He heard and received you into His kingdom.

This is a blind faith kind of thing, or better

yet, a childlike faith. It's a kid trusting his or her father (in this case God) enough to try something that seems unclear or maybe even a little scary. Let me give you another story that may help illustrate this concept.

Jump Off

Growing up in Cincinnati, we had very cold winters. Only the summer months were warm enough for us to be outside and enjoy the swimming pool. Most communities like ours had swim clubs. This is where many families got together and utilized one large pool complex. Ours had a large six-lane pool area with a separate diving area and shallow end for the smaller children. I have many happy childhood memories of hanging out at the pool—except for one.

The diving area had a one-meter diving board and a three-meter (approx. ten-foot) high diving board. I was seven years old that summer, and most of the kids my age didn't have any trouble jumping or even diving off the one-meter diving board. But the high diving board was a different story. I realized why they called it the high dive.

Most of my buddies were already going up and jumping off it. Some were even brave enough to dive off. So when I finally got the nerve to climb the ladder to the top of the three-meter board, I remember that I was scared to death of how high I was. It seemed like a hundred-meter high diving board to me.

Even though I had no problems jumping off and even diving off the one-meter board, jumping off the high dive just didn't seem possible. I thought that I would die from the impact of hitting the water from such a great height. I can't tell you the number of times that I tried to get up the nerve to jump off. I would climb to the top and slowly walk out to the end of the diving board. Then fear so overwhelmed me that I would sheepishly go back down the ladder in humiliated defeat.

What was so ironic about all this was that

I saw all my friends jumping off as if it was no big deal. No one drowned. No one got hurt. It all made total sense from my perspective on the ground to go up and try again. But for some reason, I felt that successfully surviving a jump off the high dive wouldn't work for me. It looked so appealing. The whole thing looked easy, and it made no sense that I was afraid to do it. I was just about ready to give the whole idea up when my dad intervened.

My older brother Scott finally told Dad about my whole dilemma. Dad figured he would help me accomplish the feat that was holding me back from the joy that I saw in the faces of my friends who were able to do it. So after dinner one evening, Dad announced that the whole family was going to the pool for an evening swim. As usual, the pool was not very crowded in the evenings, so Dad asked me if I would like to try to jump off the high dive with his help.

I wondered, *How can he possibly help me?* Dad said that he would be in the water below the board and promised that nothing would happen to me. He said that I would finally succeed in jumping off.

I went out to the end of the board and with blind faith (literally, because I closed my eyes) and childlike trust in my father, I jumped. I hit the water, went under for a few seconds, and when I came up, I was in my dad's arms, safe and extremely happy.

Here are some parallels between this story and being saved.

1) It all looks good and makes sense. It seems so easy.
2) I've seen and heard of others who have done it. They are people whom I know and trust.
3) I wanted to experience the joy of doing it for myself as I saw my friends enjoying it.
4) I think I'm ready, but I'm afraid that it won't work for me.
5) I think I'll wait until another time.

6) My dad (and God) promised that it would work and that I'd be ok. And that He would be there waiting for me to take the plunge.

7) The exhilarating feeling of coming up (praying the prayer of salvation) and realizing it worked.

8) My earthly father (and God) did exactly what He promised He would do.

So, are you ready to jump off and pray the prayer of salvation for yourself? Let's do it. The prayer works this way. We're going to pray using the previous steps.

1) We acknowledge God.

2) We express our need.

3) We admit our sin.

4) We ask Him to save us, to come in, and take over.

We are going to follow the exact prayer that Gil and I prayed back in 1972. Gil prayed a traditional prayer. I prayed my own version as I followed his lead. They are both side by side for your reference. You can use either one, but I suggest that you use both as you pray down the list. When you ask God to save you at the end of the prayer, it is very important that you ask God to come in and take over your life. This shows your total surrender to Him.

Please, please, please remember, God is listening to your heart and not to your words. If you're not sincere in this prayer, nothing will happen. If you are sincere, get ready to start a new life.

The Prayer of Salvation

First Ingredient:
Acknowledging God

Traditional Prayer
"Dear Heavenly
Father"

My Prayer
"God"

Second Ingredient:
Expressing Your Need

Traditional Prayer
"We come to You
seeking to get to
know You."

My Prayer
"I know that I don't
know You and
would like to."

Third Ingredient: Admitting Your Sin Nature

Traditional Prayer

"We come before You, admitting that we have sinned against You and that we need You to forgive us for all our unrighteous thoughts and deeds, which we have done throughout our lives."

My Prayer

"All I know is that I've pretty much made a mess of my life so far and that I am very sorry."

Fourth Ingredient: Asking God to Save You

Traditional Prayer

"We ask on the authority of Your Son, Jesus Christ, who died on the cross in our place, to please forgive us for all our sins."

My Prayer

"God, please forgive me and tell me what to do."

Asking God to Come in and Take Over Your Life

Traditional Prayer

"We ask that You be received into our hearts, and by Your loving Grace, I ask You to save me. Amen."

My Prayer

"God, if You want me, You can have me. I would like nothing better than for You to take over my life from now on."

It's the same prayer with different words. It brings the same results – salvation.

Reference Verses

Trust in the Lord with all your heart and lean not on your own understanding. (Proverbs 3:5 NIV)

I praise you, Father, Lord of heaven and earth, because you have hidden these things from the wise and intelligent and have revealed them to infants. (Matthew 11:25 CSB)

For God so loved the world that He gave His one and only Son, that whoever believes in him shall not perish but have eternal life. (John 3:16 NIV)

For whoever calls on the name of the Lord shall be saved. (Romans 10:13 NKJV)

Truly my soul finds rest in God; my salvation comes from Him. (Psalm 62:1 NIV)

4th Ingredient

He saved us and called us to a holy life—not because of anything we have done, but because of His own purpose and grace. (2 Timothy 1:9 NIV)

For the Son of Man came to seek and to save the lost. (Luke 19:10 NIV)

For you are receiving the end results of your faith, the salvation of your souls. (1 Peter 1:9 NIV)

FIFTH INGREDIENT
EXPECT A RESULT
God Will Let You Know That He Has Done This

"I Did It!"

These are my favorite three words to hear someone say, even more than, "I love you." or, "Dinner is ready." I hope this is you right now. Congratulations! It wasn't that hard, was it?

Salvation Beaker

Expect a Result

Ask God to Save You

Admit Your Sinful Nature

Express Your Need for God

Acknowledge God

I can't tell you how many times I have shared God's plan of salvation and have told people my story. They may respond right there on the spot, but most often, they tell me that they'll think about it. Then I see them sometime later, and they come running up to me, saying, "I did it!" I know immediately what they mean. It still thrills me to see someone do this. I helped someone meet God. Wow!

Actually, I also need to have faith when I share God's plan of salvation with someone. I often think, *What if it doesn't work this time?* But it always does. I still don't know how it works. It just does.

Now What Do I Do?

Hopefully, you were expecting a result and got one. You should now *know* that you are connected to God because His Spirit came in and filled the God-shaped space in your soul. This is your guarantee that God has restored you to a new relationship with Him. God has cleaned house by

forgiving you of all your sins. He has given you
a fresh new spiritual birth. Here is a Bible verse
that describes this:

Repent, then, and turn to God, so that your sins may
be wiped out, that times of refreshing may come from
the Lord. (Acts 3:19 NIV)

So how do you feel now? Hopefully, your
answer is the same as mine when Gil first
asked me. Great! Now, let's do a few things to
finalize what has just happened to you. There is
a specific Bible verse after each point. These are
all important steps that are suggested to help you
begin this new journey with God.

1) Thank God for Saving You

Thank Him for doing what He promised that He
would do. You just jumped into one of the biggest
faith experiences that you've probably ever had in
your life.

Though you have not seen him, you love him; and
even though you do not *see* him now, you believe in

him and are filled with an inexpressible and glorious
joy, for you are receiving the end result of your faith,
the salvation of your souls. (1 Peter 1:8-9 NIV)

2) Tell Another Christian (Believer) What You've Done

This is an important step. If this experience was
real for you, you will want to tell someone. God
wants us to verbally express what He has done.
Maybe it will be to the person who gave you this
book or someone in the past who shared God's
plan when you weren't ready to receive it. They
would be thrilled to know that you finally did it.

If you declare with your mouth "Jesus Is Lord", and
believe in your heart that God raised Him from the
dead, you will be saved. (Romans 10:9 NIV)

3) Get Plugged In

Get someone to point you in the right direction
regarding how to find a church that focuses on

this salvation experience as the main starting point of the Christian faith. Most communities have a church like this one. They are often referred to as *fundamental* Christian churches.

Now you are the body of Christ, and each one of you is a part of it. (1 Corinthians 12:27 NIV)

4) Start Reading the Bible

This is important. As I did, you now need to start reading the Bible and learning more about what has happened to you—the how, why, and what of God's overall plan for you. This also means getting yourself a Bible if you don't have one.

So then faith comes by hearing and hearing by the word of God. (Romans 10:17 NKJV)

5) Baptism

I had to ask someone to explain this one to me. I wanted to do what God had asked me to do.

Therefore, we were buried with him by baptism into death, in order that, just as Christ was raised from the dead by the glory of the Father, so we too may walk in newness of life. (Romans 6:4 CSB)

I wasn't too crazy about doing any kind of formal ceremonies, as I had had enough of that growing up in church. I had already been baptized as a child, which didn't mean anything to me looking back on it as a young adult. My (new) pastor had to explain the reason for being baptized as a believer verses a child.

First of all, the baptism that is described in the Bible is called "believer's baptism". When we are infants, baptism has no meaning for us. God wants us to get up in front of a group of fellow believers and tell them what happened when we prayed and claimed our gift of salvation.

Instead, we do a simple ceremony and act it out like a short play. Basically, you buried your sins (in a watery grave), and you were saved or rescued from death by God raising you (coming out of the watery grave) from the spiritual death that we all deserved. You are now a new creature, and you have a new life. You have been reborn. Your basically letting others know "I did it!" God knew that most of us were not public speakers, so he let us act this out in a simple play act.

It is also a public display that may encourage others, including unbelievers. It shows how serious and appreciative you are of what God has done for you.

We were therefore buried with him through baptism into death in order that, just as Christ was raised from the dead through the glory of the Father, we too may live a new life. (Romans 6:4 NIV)

6) Sharing Your Story

You will have a desire to tell others about what has happened to you, and that's awesome. It's natural because of what has just happened to you. Don't be surprised if people won't respond or can't understand what you're telling them. You have a unique story just like I do. When you share it, people may not get it at first, but they will see a change in you and know that something special has happened in your life. It's called planting a seed. This is what happens when we share our message of God's salvation.

Someone shared this with my friend Sally, and Sally shared it with me. My brother Brian saw that something had happened to me and had to find it for himself. I've seen him pass it on to so many others. On and on, the message goes. You are going to share it with someone.

But you shall receive power when the Holy Spirit has come upon you; and you shall witness to me in Jerusalem, and in all of Judea and Samaria, and to the end of the earth. (Acts 1:8 NKJV)

7) Redirecting Your Life

Remember that this prayer of salvation permanently connects you to God. He will show you how He wants you to live through Him. You will still have some of your old sin nature. You can still choose to ignore Him or follow Him. But as far as eternity is concerned, your security is intact.

The rest of your life, you will be learning how to be more like the person He wants you to become. Perfection is actually an impossible goal, but He wants you to be like Jesus as much as possible. In other words, you're saved, forgiven, and a new person (born-again), but you won't be perfect until you get to heaven.

If we confess our sins, He is faithful and just to forgive us of our sins and to cleanse us from all unrighteousness. (1 John 1:9 NKJV)

I think you will find these steps helpful in beginning your new spiritual life. I can still remember the first time that I told other people, who had done the same thing, that I was saved. They knew exactly what I was talking about, without my having to explain it. Yet trying to tell my story to someone who wasn't a believer, sometimes resulted in them looking at me like I was crazy. They didn't have a clue what I was talking about.

Do you remember in the beginning of this experiment when I asked if you could put aside all your unanswered questions? Well, now that you have the God of the universe inside you, do you really care if any of them are answered? Don't you feel that God knows the answer to everything and that we can just let Him deal with it? We'll find out someday (if not here, then in heaven) how everything fits together. Personally, that's good enough for me.

Enjoy your new life. Welcome to the kingdom. I may never meet you here, but I'm sure we'll have plenty of time in eternity to reminisce about how we did this experiment together.

God loves you, and so do I.

I'LL TAKE MY CHANCES

So you have decided that you're not going to pursue this salvation experiment. You're going to take your chances and accept the consequences that may be yours upon death. I'm interested in your reasons for this decision. Which one of these best describes your decision?

1) I can't accept that there is only one way to connect with God.
2) I do not want to be grouped with the hypocritical Christians that I know.
3) I have put too much time and effort into my current religious beliefs to change.

4) I have done the best I can with my life, and if that's not good enough, I'll take my chances.

5) I feel that my good deeds far outweigh my bad ones. I believe God will tilt the balance in my favor.

6) I believe God is love, and if that's true, He cannot and will not turn away from me.

Of course, all these are self-conceived and are not God-initiated ideas.

One thing that we all can agree on is that once we die, we cannot come back and change our minds about salvation. We have one life and one opportunity to decide whether this is what we should or shouldn't invest in, check out, or pursue.

Someday when you face God and He asks you why you didn't receive His message of salvation (His offer for you to come into a right relationship with Him), what will you say? You cannot say that you did not know or have the opportunity. This book is one of those opportunities. It may be a final opportunity.

You also might be politely thinking, *Well, good for you. I'm glad you found something positive in your life.*

Let me present an interesting scenario about this comment. Let's just say that you're right, and I'm wrong about this whole salvation thing. That it's not true and I'm wrong for thinking that it's the only way to God. I say there's no harm done. My reason? It's because I have a belief that I have connected with God. If nothing else, I've lived my life with some good guidelines and a hope for my eternal future.

But if I'm right, and you're wrong, I'm going to be okay after I leave this earth, and you may have a not-so-good eternity. Think about that. I'm a winner either way. I have nothing to lose.

Remember, this decision is made while you're here on Earth and not afterward. You still have an opportunity to reconsider.

If not, good luck.

I would love to hear from you.
Please write me at:

Tom Stegeman
16295 S. Tamiami Trail, # 230,
Fort Myers, Fl. 33908

You can also visit our website for more
information, videos and resources at:
www.afinalexperiment.com